Bodies of Wood and Water

Bodies of Wood and Water

Poems by

Kirk S. Westphal

Kelsay Books

Cover art by Cris Perez

ISBN: 978-1-947465-71-8

Kelsay Books
Aldrich Press
www.kelsaybooks.com

For
My Lady, and My Lake

Acknowledgements

Dunes Review: "Bodies of Water," "Footprints in December," "This," "Day's Work," "Holding Her," "Read This Twice," "After Reading," "Weight of Air," "Asking Forgiveness," "Eden," "Beneath a Bridge."
Albatross: "The Dance"
The Road Not Taken: "Our Room"

"Consecration" first appeared as the Poem of the Month on the website for an organic farm in Harvard, Massachusetts—*Old Frog Pond Farm*: http://oldfrogpondfarm.com.

"Curvatures of Earth" first appeared in the chapbook *Lines in the Landscape*, a collection of winning poems from the Plein Air Poetry Contest in Massachusetts sponsored by Fruitlands Museum and the Concord Poetry Center, 2012.

I wish to thank the poets and friends who have read me through these words, and steered me clear of the shoals: Jack Ridl, D.R. James, Mark Seiler, Anastasia Townsend, Melissa Fournier, Rob Astor, Georgia Sassen, George Clark, and Franny Osman. To past and present editors of Dunes Review in Traverse City, Jennifer Yeatts and Tanya Muzumdar, thank you for the platform on the page and at the podium—a place to share my voice with so many inspiring writers and readers. I also thank my friend Dave, who taught me the forest and its trees. And to my teenage children, Ben and Ellie, who tease me mercilessly about writing lyrical poetry, thank you—you inspire me all the more.

Contents

The ancients called man a lesser world, and certainly the use of this name is well bestowed, because his body is an analog for the world ... the lungs rise and fall in breathing, so the body of the earth has its ocean tide which likewise rises and falls every six hours, as if the world breathed.

—Leonardo Da Vinci

Bodies of Water

If I was Sky and you were Lake,
arching over, slipping under
we would wake and we would sleep
always facing one another.
We would replenish.
I would fill your depths
and you would breathe warm vapor
into my mouth.
My white and grey have been you,
Your grey and blue have been me,
and in between the colors
liquid questions rise and fall
in shapes of crescents waiting
to hold their answers—
    How, then, did we ever live *before*?

I would see my sun-fired brim
reflected deep within you,
stirred now what in me alone was still,
and you would tell me it had always been there,
just as your white birds have always leaned
into the currents of my wind.
And I would rest against you softly,
knowing that *before* never existed.

Consecration

I am the fallen hemlock
beside the trail,
dry rot pulp and moss breath,
the naked ribcage of my sins
spindling outward at incomplete angles
remembering the heavy lattice
of their green-black days.
Please, as you pass by,
break off a branch each day.
Snap it to the trunk,
in pieces if you must, leaving nothing
so that one day I may rest here
proud as a mainmast
or as the noble elegy
of some great spire.

Footprints in December

Shelf ice from the banks
flattens above black water,
the year runs out beneath, and sighs
while I sip the breath of sparrows.
My feet leave imprints in
compliant hummocks,
dark crystal in sugar snow.
Across and upstream, earlier,
beneath the leafless skeletons
a young boy with blond hair
stands with a trembling bluebird
in his outstretched hands,
cupped and lifted
to protect, but to show me.
His eyes, the same hearth-dark as winter,
same as mine have always been.
He turns without footprints,
leaving just the blue on black and white,
and the river pours this cold year into next.

Tender

If you live in the north
you may wake one deep night
at two o'clock to discover
that your furnace is out
and that outside, the frost
cakes in single digits,
brittling through cracks
in the old windows.

You will see your breath
in the stairwell telling you
to shoulder first your coat
and then as many logs as you can
trundle through the deep.
Your forearms will strain,
remembering the hoisted maul,
now hauling wood before its time.

You will start a fire
and protect it all night
as if you were watching
for the subtle flare of nostrils
or the rising chest of a sleeping newborn.

And you will run the faucets gently
so the pipes outrun the frost,
and you will not sleep until

the fire breathes steadily
and the water runs evenly,
quietly, without a rattle.

The fragile flow of elements,
And you, the tender.

This

She shows me water from a distance,
smoothes its folds to glass
and sets our table—
our plates two islands,
berries in a bowl of sweetwater mint,
the incense of our pining hands.
Our bread is just the courage
of these outcrops.
Forks as feathers.
I ask what she would like to drink
and she answers,
"This."

If Ever I Build a Church

I will use red cedar,
calm forgiveness the scent
and lifeblood of every beam,
and in it I will light a candle
in the name of the one tree
that stood proudly on the misty hill
just down the tracks
outreaching the other cedars
until the day I felled it, limbed it,
hitched it to my waist and hauled it
down the trail with knotted muscle
and some rope
and stacked its bleeding boards
outside my open window where
for days they purified my house
with incense
before rising again
as an auburn paneled door, a way,
and a lofty ridge pole at the apex
of a space made otherwise
from pine and oak and cherry
long since dead.
And I would kneel in this church
seeking absolution
for revealing the spirit,
having worn the breastplate
of the Centurion
breaking the flesh.

Day's Work

Grey reveals the air again,
thick enough to ply
and laden with the palpitations
of yesterday's wake.
Dark was cold but now I move about.
The cold is why I work today
and why my wings unfold
with a weak, uncertain crack.
Before I scavenge enough fill
we are gathered, suddenly aloft, a burst
of stiff unready flight
and feeling more of bone than feather
I press my way into the vee
and now again the everything below
moves but never changes.
Hypnotic draft and undulation,
those ahead and to the left pull
as if the lift and thrust of body wings
is divined by some spirit
of chains and sprockets
and we pray this something
to hold aloft our form above this ache
and to let us feel again the brush
beneath our chin, along our neck,
for though we fly with oiled precision,
we forget each day what it is to fly
until the Grey returns and calls us down

and I unfurl into the billow of air
then water then Dark
then me.
Tomorrow we work again
toward another ending.

Cabin Trilogy

I. Leathered

These hands prepare for work,
leathering their palms and oiling their knuckles
with the tannins and the warm sap of hardwoods.
I'll put my books aside awhile
because my hands want only the shanks
of grey-cracked wood and iron,
the axe, the saw, the Peavey
made for men with the chests and shoulders
and foreheads of oxen.
And these hands will raise from weathered trees
a shelter
strong enough to bend back rain
and soft enough to hold you here.
They will cut and haul, crack and bleed,
steady my back and break my fall,
raise a glass of rough whiskey
then wipe the evening brow.
And when they once again lay down their tools
I will wash them with tea leaves
and they, too, will be
soft enough to hold you here.

II. Cups

You spread the morning forest at our feet,
You dip your hands into the valley bowl

and press a dewberry into my mouth,
You draw the river mist through umber soil
   and pour it in our cups—
Earthen cups we bought
with the blue-glazed bowl
to hold this day until it wakes,
to hold the first taste of this mountain.
I'll make the bed if you make breakfast.

III. Window

A life already lived,
it gathers dust and cobwebs
on flaccid panes that once collected light.
It lit a thousand days of rest,
ten thousand more of work,
and all the days of fever.
At night it spilled a family's embers
on the leaves outside,
then spread butter on the morning bread
in quiet preparation.
When we find it forgotten
behind crisp and peeling plywood
or old apple crates in a barn,
and mount it in the kitchen
as the keystone of our space,
it will fill our days

with the light of a thousand cities,
bronze our wood and warm our bread,
then share our embers with the owls.

Body of Water

O, River, will you dance with me
the song of our own composition?
Turn to me and quench my thirst,
   our bodies chest to chest.

My River, curl your eddy breath
around my neck and shoulder muscles,
Pour our Names from one deep sigh,
   the watershed exhales.

And River, turn me in your palm
between your silver sheets of rain,
burnish me, meander me,
   and lift me from the stones.

O, River, take me under now,
in robes of our evaporation,
take my breath, emulsified,
   your Current now am I.

Then River, as your rain I'll fall,
remember how my aspect faced you,
how I hummed your fluvial runes,
   and tumbling, learned the Dance.

*This poem was written in memory of a young man, Max, who was killed by a
hit–and–run driver in the Arizona desert. Max lived with the Hopi people,
helping them grow corn. The Hopi believe that the spirits of the departed return
to them as rain—their sustenance.*

The Dance

Out among the trees past midnight
moonlight and wood smoke
speak in ether tongues

"Why is it you love me?" asks the smoke.

"You turn me into rivers,
  Without you I am still."

"And you, you hold me buoyant,
the weight of light is our discretion."

"You fill the space between the branches
  with my wishes."

"I was once a tree like these
and knew your soft caress.
I chose to die to find you."

"I saw you then but could not taste you.
  Now I sip you slowly."

"I flow across your lips
in the patterns of the grain
I knew beneath but never saw."

"And we become the shape and color
   of water."

"And the sound of pearls
underneath all currents."

   "Do you miss standing?"

"I am no longer afraid to fall."

   "I used to whisper on your shoulder
      hoping you would hear."

"I felt the silver of your breath."

   "I was asking if one day
      you would dance with me."

Wolving Hour

Waking mists, edge of nakedness,
when vapor sheets recede
under cover of grey
as sleep's sublimation
into glasswater dawn,

Dream-ghosts almost now forgotten,
steal away, lupus laminar
converging on a singularity
out upon the lake, just beyond
the sunlight's gracious hesitation
to be mollified by their own evaporation,
their frozen breath
possessed, possessing.

They wisp away the frailties too heavy
for my waking lungs to bear.

White Space

A single limb suspends
each appled blush and blemish,

With cider hope they breathe
the sightlines of this honest orchard,

Thankful for the even air between rows,
no tree hides nor boasts.

A pause between words
unfolds the shade among them.

Alight in the margins
before the harvest.

Conversation

Not as much the soil as the air
or the hummingbird's brief palpitation
in it, swimming

Not as much the walls of field stone
as the sculpted shapes and sounds within
that trust them

Not as much the tea leaf as the temperature
that cures an earthbound essence
into steam

Not as much the willow as its shade
of feather-paper
patient as honey

Not as much the bluebird as its pallet
and its brushstrokes liquifying
frozen air

Not as much the organ as the silence
in the stone-still chapel
remembering the coda

Not as much the season as the knowledge
it will settle
in omniscience

Not as much the movement as the dance,
the body as a tongue dipping slowly
into salt

Not as much the river as the reverence
of its thousand rivulets
beneath the boughs

    Not as much the words as their containment
    and their visage—
    Our speaking to each other

Fractals

Promontory porch
upward and away,
as pulpit or as pew
in this, our midnight sanctuary
viscous with the silver milk of moon sheets
rippling through the stone still pines
whose trunks divide
  to boughs dividing
    into branches
      into sprigs and
       into needles
which etch the silver,
black as night would be without the moon
each dendrite slender as the clock hand
noticed only for its stillness
and medieval demarcations of its shape.
Our words become the trunk and
  bough,
    branch and
      sprig, and then,
       the tiny needles
hanging, reaching,
so clearly etched against unrippled light,
yet soft enough to remember the tanager's voice.

My Lady, My Lake

I cast my eyes across your rise and fall
until I see beneath your linen wavelets
to soft sand glades where drops of light
   shimmy, quiver, emulsify
to places where artful refraction
   bends them away
   so that you alone may know the writhe
   and hunger of your secrets,
   and may keep them sheltered
   by the mystic round of each soft crescent
   bending into shadow
Show me the surge of life beneath your skin,
   all that draws its breath from you,
Look back at me,
Undress me, too,
My Lady, My Lake.

Holding Her

I may build a wooden canoe
so I would come to know
how the soft caress of water
can bend wood,
and so I might know
the bones and skin of such a shape,
know its ribs with my palms
and understand with my fingers
how the ache of any curve
is the seeking of another
and becoming it,
and I would gently grip the gunwales
as she slipped or slept beneath me,
holding her still
or easing her through waves.

Maker's Longing

Born to carve my name into valleys,
emulsion of sun and rain,
I am my Maker's longing
to meander and to oxbow,
to sculpt and acquiesce,
to know the land above
and to the sides
and wonder with enduring ache
what lies below.

Currents

Knotted pine,
timber waves of grain
around an imperfection, not a blemish,
once a living branch
that reached and breathed
and traded shade for water,
child first, then parent,
an etching now of river-burnished stones,
an umber story told in full,
polished, tanned
by patient streamlines of forgiveness
that beautify each stem of life in elegy.

Outside a room of pine-board walls
the mighty Androscoggin turns the river stones
while children ramble in the woods.

Read This Twice

Beginnings ask with fingers
clutching, coaxing, tracing,
holding as to guide
but formed around the shape of water,
eyes that sweat before first contact
spin and drift, beholden to themselves
and what they touch
within a sphere of imminence,
portent firm as shoulders
squaring now to their encounter,
their potency affirmed as still life
in rotation and intention—
yet hips will lead this heat dance
pivot first then thrust
the body's leather angles
into curves as smooth as wood grain,
each its own expectant contour
of the body as a helix of desire.
Fingers tighten
   eyes commit the hips
     into gyration
        spiraling to shoulders ...
Contact without feeling any threshold
no before nor after and
the need itself suppresses all resistance.
And so it goes—the baseball sails into forever,
sphere of imminence now permanence.
To hit it is to swing clear through.

Patience: Great Lakes Hydrology

Freshet

A droplet falls on faint indifferent earth
the soil moistens, grateful, yet it boasts
that fleeting imprints pass along, away
to climes where thirst is mightier than now
in rivulet, at first, transparent veins
of currents and alliances unnamed,
convergence, muted buoyancy midstream—
the shallows of ephemeral mystique.

Confluence

The molecules of millions intercede
each duty bound to self, and self to God
with vast indifference yet to unknown ends
the sweat of slope and swale, as such it goes
now rising to the current combing air
and pulling it along for casual breath
then dipping down through verdant mirror glass
to temperatures below of self-same hue.
The pools and riffles of a transiency,
venturi, oxbow, always straight ahead,
through canyon swath of those who long ago
began collecting geologic grains
that crystallize to clarity and hue

as they dissolve-infuse time's father-rock
to hydrologic minutes scouring by
who, sightless but to round the bend ahead
resolve to sound the measurable depth
of their affirmed immediacy here.

Estuary

The banks that once protective coasted by
recede and part as elemental wrists
behind, resolved as open hands that now
release to hemispheres of blue beyond
while currents' pull remembered slides away
beneath, dispersion of ideals conveyed
as motion rounding pebbles on its way
to here, to uncut earth or none at all
amidst a new stratigraphy of self
as soluble as salts too faint to taste,
collected proverbs scoured and repressed.

Open Water

Until with shores too distant to be seen,
a chance to sigh and weep, be one with gales
or sink to safer depths below, and yet,

the risk of vapor, spindrift life above
too rich in its allure to shun the light
and so it gathers upward, crest to crest
it may remain a year or hundreds hence
as sage-grey eddies spin in current's wake
and choosing to exist where light may reach
its seasons will enumerate with ice
however many crystal chances wait.

Straits

Then chapters, seasons, eons fold away
as funneled truths conspire to reveal
an archipelago of lakes—it asks
how blue, how cold, how deep the next may be,
what tints of ice await, how coarse the shore?
No answer in reply, and so it goes
and passing to the next, now recognized
as glacial echoes, nowhere such as these
are joined in sequence, fresh, and cosmic vast
delineated by the curve of earth
where blue disguised as grey resolves to green
beneath its surface lens, and so it goes.

Basins

A hundred years may pass again away
as lake to planet lake in slow cascade,
Superior's ancestral ice warms south,
as scoured cliffs survey its arctic pace
through maritime mystique, November shoals,
and currents of its topaz-pebbled shore
to join with Michigan's white sand adjourned
from dune grass hill and shallow viscous steppe
with borrowed brilliance from Petoskey suns
in shadows of the lighthouse galleries
that spread a prairie wind across the waves
toward Huron's bays like gulfs contained as coves
so vast that necklaces of light are lost
around the rim of concave heaving chest
that breathes to buoy vessels and their heft,
the bounty of the land where rivulets
might sacrifice to capillary dreams,
then through the throat of rusted industry
to Erie's furnace gone to verdant flower.
peninsulas and jetties reach as hands
extending invitations here to rest.
In each of these the droplet, pure distills
into the fragrance of freshwater known
to those who dwell in this hydrology,
an offering of tea leaves in the mist.

Passage

Acceleration, tumult waves arise
in fellowship or conquest? Currents charged
with rapid heaving lungs that breathe the flow
of upland lakes inhaled now to pause
and exhaled to the brink of mighty vow,
the precipice of cataract ahead
and so it goes, and so it knows the life
it lived has not been passive vanity
but knowledge of a glorious return
to mists that rise again from plunging joy
at having now arrived at water's edge …
where every water droplet longs to be.
And so the colors gathered on its way
in gratitude for passage safe and full
combine into a namesake hue so pure

it sings a final aqua-psalm above
and with this prayer of transcendental thanks
itself and all its hues surrendered full
its trust, its final offering in white
over the edge now sighs, yet rises still …
Niagara's mist, a freshet yet to come.

What is it About This Fish

I hold in my hands?
He looks at me—I know he sees.
He suffers, gasps for breath
and yet I cannot let him go
just yet,
this envy trying not to become lust.
My palms know the dormant strength
and desire beneath his scales.
Holding him just above the water
is not unlike touching a woman
for the first time.
How hard must I press to hold?
How tender to suspend?

Maybe it is this:
the Mind as one Muscle,
to rise or fall by wishing it,
or maybe this:
the writhe and desperation of
the Muscle as its Mind,
the unity, and nothing more.

I hold him so he sees me,
the knowing glance of rivals,
he, the wiser of the two,
having learned to feather his spirit
in the glide.

Maybe I want him to know this,
or perhaps he just wished
to tell me.

Just like that, and away.

Seaworthy

A parting of the waters in the trees,
bending back away a curtain of the wind and rain waves
with the plunging wooden French curves of her bow—
Handmade woodshed, that is all,
shanty song of hammer, mine
and dulcet wheeze of saw blades
carving timbers from the scent of drying leaves
and wood smoke.
Plain dimensions, eight by twelve
but hefty draft,
stowage for the premonitions of my sweaty tools
and empty paint can barnacles.
Voyage of the yet to be and was.
Her timbers I first knew as forest—
I, as jack and wood wright was their death
or resurrection, believing as I do in both

Cedar on the windward hill, did you know
that as the mainmast you'd unfurl our sails proudly
as the billow of deep fresh snow on the pitched roof?

Cherry, blanched and crooked in the woodlot,
limbs that doubt or shrug away the promiscuity of spring,
reveal your musk and grain as deck boards
spread beneath the tannins of the sun, above the wash—

Or is dignity in standing as your own elegiac spire?
What I know is that her hull and bulwarks,
Rough-hewn boreal sea salt pine
has mixed with sweat and with my sawdust spit
to be a place that had not been,
as fit as any vessel on the sea,
where I am captain.

Paper

We write our nightsong
on a warm papyrus sky—
our words meander until meeting
at the midspan of the bridge,
suspended there as
the slowdance of fireflies,
the vowels of our open mouths
By morning they lay themselves
on river's linen sheets—
We may gather them
and make this bed.

The Keepers

Reverent hands select boards
that will hold the books,
Poplar, neither hard nor soft—
the durability of words
and malleability of intentions
embossed with clear grain of a Vermont river,
shadowed with alluring verdant hues
exposed to light
after years of quiet preparation
in the lexicology of trees.
These boards might have become paper
but do not choose their resurrection
nor measure one against another.
Ink on paper smells as new and old
as a fresh saw cut—
no knots in finely crafted lines.

After Reading

Inspired by Quan Barry's *Reading*

Night took me home
the long way—

along the nowhere canal,
beside the familiar street
I cannot name

toward awareness
and the eloquence of silence
after speaking.

Casting

If I were the River that you fished,
tell me where you'd cast your line—

In the shallows at your feet
where I shed the scoured days of dust?

In the eddies of my self-awareness
where a strike is sure but callow?

In my midriff current
where the way is clear, but only downstream?

Or toward the hollows of the far shore
where the great shadows skulk in reverie

but where your line may tangle in the roots
and snap?

If you lift the strength of a fish from my waters,
Will it prostrate into supple in your hands?

Prunus Serotina

Have You smelled the wood of a cherry tree,
Fresh cut, reborn in umber musk,
Finding purpose renewed?

Have Your fingertips danced on its seasoned grain
Of strings strung tight on varnished wood,
Releasing clear, rich tones?

Have You climbed its strong unraveling branches,
Felt their embrace while ascending,
Wrapped with silken white hands?

Have You tasted its succulent lifeblood fruit,
Picked fresh from its stem with your lips,
To mix its essence with yours?

Can You open Your eyes from this to see
Your own light draped over seasons,
Finding form, renewing leaves?

Sea of Glass

The mainsail should have been reefed
in the harbor,
Now I lean on transom stern
while runes upon the brittle swell
fracture around an insolent bow.
In the cabin glasses rattle,
a book spills all over the floor.
The gaff salutes its captain wind.

Safe away from deepwater shoals
the now translucent shards collect
in the cusp of upturned shells,
water wounds within a blown glass bulb
preserved yet smoothed
and rounded patiently
for me to gather.

Herb Garden

In the upper bedroom my eyes hang low
like mist through the wet green of morning forest,
as she stoops over the hearth below
where her Mother planted Mary's Rose
and where her Father laid the sage stones,
where the wind off the sweet bay settles,
drawing up the slope of grass dripping lemon
into rising air of sun dew,
and where, through her folds of lavender
I can see she gathers time in her hands.

Mountain Stream

As mist between the cedars
you may hear me,
sound beneath Time,
shaman to the wind,
oxygen in high Sierra veins.
My April gasp and autumn sigh
slowly wind the clock tower trees
with insouciant precision,
that they may know each passing year,
because to them it matters.
I unspool the fisherman
into riffling incantations of his lust,
above and below all octaves.
I am the Mobius curve
of a meadowlark's song
if she whispered it outside
your open window at sunrise.

Northern Mountains

Fresh streams of crystal thought distill a truth
that undulation's heft may still all thoughts
for now as balsam pathways forage, climb
up into clouds and lakes that they have wrought,
Where moon reveals itself as slivered light
that silhouettes a ridge in its ascent
above the valleys that through time protect
upheaval as a virtue, heaven bent,
Whose gradients are traced by wanderers
whose purpose, washed and cooled by mountain rain
reveals itself in quiet steps or heaves.
We may pass through but footfalls will remain.

    Through valleys, ridges, chisled chasms, clefts,
    I see my grain and know my frail heft.

From Frost's Front Porch

Beyond these posts of wooden white
inclined toward spruce-capped summits south
I part my lips into the height
where proud ravine conceals its light
but pours its secret in my mouth.

My feet have seen it, and my eyes,
where streams begin and are begun
by sipping saturated skies
'til rock and vapor spill as one

from firmament terrestrial
all elementals pure dissolve
to hills and skin ancestral,
and all my minerals absolve.

For upward from here and away,
aware what thirsty steps have sought,
the stunted boughs will light my way
and granite will my heels stay
but I need water as my thought.

Taken

She remembers the soldiers
returning from the South
in slop-step rags
before she could bear apples for them.

A thousand winds have dressed her
and then stripped her bare.

She knows each coat of paint
beside her on this aged house
and every ghost and every
child's name gathered
in the pink shade of low abiding branches—

Even mine, her last.
In her place a new pipe and scarred earth,
the unfinishing of her story.

I am not a Fisherman, but I am a Man Who Fishes

And just beyond dusk
I hook a bass in the middle of the lake.
He flings himself twice above the surface,
writhing in the revelation of his form and will
but concealing his colors,
Just the outline of muscle on silver black,
sipping for a moment my same air,
tethered to each other
with a gossamer ephemerality,
His gasps to my transgression,
His full strength to the temperance in my forearms,
Until he slips the hook
and is away.

Woodsman in a White Shirt

I leaf through papers, briefs,
opinions and facts outseasoning each other
and forgetting themselves
while I roll up my shirtsleeves
so that the pen in my grip
might fall more nimbly
into the proper angle of their grain,
quarter them with wit,
and stack them in the corner of dusky intellect
before the cold.
As I turn the cuffs
they feel a bit like flannel, red on black,
and the air chills just enough
that through my breath
the sturdy handle of my hatchet
finds its old parched fingers
and becomes the sureness in my shoulders—

Anyway, there's work to be done.

The Lake Within

She is away
and with weary words she called
to say good night from a sailboat
in its harbor,
where she was apart from the others
for a while at dusk.
She described a female duck floating by,
alone, apart,
the shape of a slipper stepping,
her head already tucked beneath her wing
where her strength and her wounds
lie down together
on the lake within.
It is late when I realize
that she was seeing herself.

Convalescence

In a painting of a grove
with depth but no distance,
winter's floor with no ceiling,
naked trunks rise from snow
into an upward void.
I come here within myself
when my body is broken,
or when the brittle lattice
of my glassblown spirit trembles.
I seek the tree most comfortable
to lean against, if only for awhile,
and from here I cast my eyes
over the evenness of the snow,
and pray it remains
untrampled.

Angling

We speak of writing poems
as if we are telling good fishing stories—
"I got one out of this, or that."

Lakesworth of shadows and reflections
and we in our small, slight skiffs
believing that we know the spot

while watching purity stream by
unable to lift it with our hands
until it rises, choosing us

then gasps for breath until
we call it forth or cast it back,
its eyes return our own intrepid hesitation

We may be terrified to touch it
but the writhe and desperation of live muscle
in our palm, almost erotic, flesh beneath iridescent scales—

I went North to the Great Waters
to join my fellow anglers round a table
and look … I got one.

Let me Become your Favorite Tree

where my leaves drip sponge light
on your cheek,
and where my shade will keep
the auburn secret of your hair
for later seasons.
Climb past my hips and up my spine
where all my strength is gathered
for my shoulders to divide,
feel the silent surge of muscle
underneath the paper bark,
and peel it back to free the forest musk,
be the first to burnish with your hands
an unseen grain.
Paint me before the seasons drain my color,
and in learning their shapes and shadows,
come to trust my limbs
to protect the delicacy of eggshells.

Sediment

Summer is the flood tide
submerging the city in its salty swilter
when even the cavities of seclusion
are filled with new particulates,
sweated through and briny.
A wave may stir and rustle us
into resuspension
only to deposit us again
into a nameless tide pool
matted with a thick, wet ambient depth,
marinating in sultry suggestions.
Languid elm leaves hang the way kelp rises.
Movement is a viscous turbid whim,
distant as the lunar seduction of spring,
as we wait for autumn's ebb.

Release and Catch

Back upward from the paleo murk
and gravity of low light
and the press of suspension
just before freezing,
through the stratified deposits
of last season's twilight,

Snap the cold air into your lungs
on the frozen lake.
You know what lies beneath,
you have been in the slurry
barely moving
among the burrowing catfish and trout,
equalized by internal instruction,

You auger a hole through the ice
and wait with open palms
for the prayer that you released below
to rise into your hands.

Paces

The river strums its psalms through the valley,
polishing the rubble of time
with reverence to gravity
and resonance in the rhapsody
of its own tumble.
It knows the forest.

The sap beside runs only in its season,
awakened by molasses incantations
through viscous sinews,
the slow dance of fluvial desire and patience.
It knows the tree.

As I walk the valley I envy
its variance in stride.

Silver Maple

Wind pulls at the hem of each quivering leaf,
lifting skirts, lapels flung wide,
no modesty prevails.

Here, underneath, the inside-out,
trees display their treasured hues
of branches leafed with coins.

They are minted in silver from green so pale,
sunlight cannot soften leaves—
they cannot help but shine.

They absorb the light of their season–life,
stored within their cells and veins,
patient in the heat

Until summer yields to harvest moon—
Summer silver, Autumn gold,
Metallic maple trees.

Weight of Air

I know what it sounds like empty
how the dust and hair thistle into wafts
and find throat-dry silence in corners
the harmonic scale of the stairway
and the crick of weight
bearing on the uprights
bone blackened into stumps
of calcified footing
Doors cling to the ratchet ache
of stolid hinges left unswung
lead-paint windows welded shut
by the absence of breeze in fallen rooms
that gurgle in the rain
as if they might be choking on it

I know what it sounds like empty
because once I heard it full

Nothing More

I am away from home—
I worked hard today
and smell of sweat,
cocktail of red wine and brine,
my body the table and
nearby sea.
A sailor's oaken scent
to seduce the heaving waves
and nothing more tonight,
the laying down
of slow-bricked hands
in the sweet pungency
of a day's work.

On Things to Forget

Forget your umbrella.

Feel the insect crawl
of droplets in your hair
scuttling beneath your collar.
To water, you are earth.

Hold the stream
at the moment of its birth
and feel its chest expand.

Let it soak your leaves,
your roots.

Then shed your sodden clothes
and lie naked on your bed
just to dry.

Our Room

In wooden room of northern pine,
Whose pervious grain retains
Three hundred years of passers by
And I am but the same.

Of coast and forest, sentry timbers
Overhead now strain
To bend the cold and rain away
From those who rest ... no names.

Beneath, a hearth in ageless stone,
Within, a quiet flame,
That warms the spirits of its guests
When they depart, before they came.

And I, I sit with One I know,
Two chairs here, both the same.
Our words pass silent in this place,
We came to leave our names

In walls that will remember long,
In floor boards that will strain
Beneath the feet of guests to come.
This wood now holds our name.

Beneath

Still pond beneath the birch and maple,
You and I are not much different.
Your leaves are new each year,
Your water fresh,
but the sediment beneath
has been forever
and we wash it only slowly
while it deepens and buries itself
in the murk.

Curvatures of Earth

Perfect is the curve
that knows its reason
and beginnings.
The honor of the trees is not to bow,
and yet baptismal waters
temper fallen trunks and limbs
to arcs, a vaulted earthen hemisphere
that in its turn
will curve the saturated sky
away from smoky tendrils
curling up from embers on the hearth
around the pillars, toward the arch,
infusing with its scent and shadow
deep beneath remaining bark
the grain of wooden time
that curves to flow around each imperfection
just as rivers round their stones.
The internal directive is redemption.
The Longhouse trees bow down again to earth,
following their grain.
Far enough is back to their beginnings.

Derivatives

Blue.
Azure afternoon
sweats an ocean
that inherits its color—
Blue descends to blue
and deepens
to a depth
where insistent light
gathers for its last dance
to shadow music
and if you look
through the blue
you will see it
clarify first
and then dissolve
to bronze
of sand beneath water
joining the dance
and running with sweat
of skin turned bronze
by the same sun
that turns the afternoon
Blue.

Borealis

Hemisphere of northern sky
pools as water
above silhouettes
of conifers climbing a boreal ridge,
upward, as if toward the light
of a pebble moon that dimples
faraway surface and ripples
the night-blue depths
into violet with its cosmic persuasion.

I saw this sky only once, on paper,
when I painted it together
with my young daughter.

Cataracts

I photographed my two young children
at the Falls, Niagara's chasm
over their narrow shoulders.
Through the tainted lens I saw
their frail bodies,
far less a match against
the weight and press
of four freshwater seas
than the sweating earth itself,
which finally yields so that
the water sheds itself and its emotion,
turning color as it does
so that it carves and sculpts below
with aqua-light.
It travels onward,
cooled and still infused.
'This is where each droplet
hopes to be,' my son remarks.
I let the camera fall to my side,
its still life captured,
and I look directly at my children
with unclouded eyes, and flowing
I see two minds, two spirits.
And the dimensions of two young lives
and the falls
trade places.

Asking Forgiveness

Fractured hummock ice on the bay this morning
any rifts that open, grey
A deepwater ship moored in frozen months
points toward open water beyond,
a compass needle, knowing.

A shorebird on the beach
could not wait long enough
and perished by the edge of hunger
or of North Wind off the bay,
now a carcass hull
becoming its own ribcage
like the old ships.

The belly of the ship groans
at ancient captive ice
knowing it has not begun to tremble
and it must before it cracks and yields
to bow waves breaking once again
across the dust of days.

Eden

I know a Bridge between an Orchard and a Lake,
between the lifting down of apple weight
and resurrection of the limbs,
between the outstretched years of applewood
and driftwood, new each morning,
One cupped hand of earth
on either side.
I sleep within the Orchard
and you beside the Lake
but it is your flesh beneath the fruit skin,
my palm beneath the waves,
your leafy eyes upon me,
my touch emulsified.
If this is Holy Water,
If these are Trees of Life,
Hands, the Bridge.
Words, the River.

Beneath a Bridge

I saw a swan sleeping at midday,
head folded from the light,
alone, not looking.
They mate for life, you know,
and so I have a thousand questions.
Did you feather her spirit to rest,
or did she just never return?
When she was here,
breakfast was called gathering.
Now it is scavenging.
Do you remember her scent
arriving before she did?
Nothing seems like yours now,
not even the River.
It is all taken.
And the space she left beside you—
what is its name?

But no, one day cygnets.
All along it was her, tending,
And so my last question is
Where are you?
You mate for life, you know.

Then one day I see you, just downriver,
swimming back,
baptized in a frail white.

Iris

Mine grows just beneath the ferns
well off the path, near the place
where the gentle persuasion of the grade
bends my footprints closer.

Her hands unfold upward
as if they once were wings,
grateful for each dropule of light
in this mossy glen.

Somehow she distills the umber green
and pine noir into violet and absinthe—
She thirsts for her color
and sighs when I taste it.

I learned where to find her
on the day the ferns unscrolled
and swore me to their secret.

And You Replied

I asked you for a glass of wine
And you poured me a pitcher of water

I asked you for a place to rest
And you pointed to a high trail

I asked your name
And you picked me a handful of cherries

I told you I was broken
And you placed a bluebird in my hands

I asked if you would like to know my name
You said you did already

I asked you how
and you led me up the trail
to an outcrop where we rested
and drank water and ate cherries
and set free the fragile bird

And as we followed it with our eyes
you whispered
The way it knows where it is going
even from this unknown stone—
That is how I know you.

Saturation

This rain does not fall gently
This torrent knows no edge of calm
but thunders down to earth's awareness,
free range tympani in octaves
Like the time we stood outside
the old white pillars
and it poured around my collar folds
and cut the gorge between my shoulder blades—
cleft of granite, new, and there to hold,
and yet to hold,
and yet to soften,
yet to moisten fertile earth
to verdancy,
to paint the lake a lighter shade,
to chant the morning vespers over fields
the rain must speak in feathers,
must find itself in rivulets
that trace the indentation of your temple
to a secret destination
where your neck becomes your cheek
without realizing it.
This pall that buttresses the thunder
also sings the mist to sleep—
Any other voice would be afraid.

Quantum Physiques

We swam across the lake that Day
when summer lolled,
leaping from our tethered valence state
into a higher orbit where being is a cloud
of probability

We lay on our bellies on the far side
in shallows of September's cove,
choosing pebbles for each other,
holding them to liquid light

And marveled at the stones, our skin,
our gravity and water holding us,
all particles whose probability of being here and now
Equaled One.

For now. For then.
We spun chances in our high elliptical suspension
before swimming back down,
releasing light.

Noah's Ark

Thousand years of sun
on million years of salt
and desert skin still sweats
its daily benediction.

If whoever you call God
asked you to build a boat
in the thousand mile drydock
of the sand,
would you boast or curse or pray?
Would you turn your back,
or turn your shoulders
to the work?
If you knew your hands would crack
and work themselves to leather
on the gossamer belief
in distant buoyancy—
On the day when God asks you
to build your boat,
will your hands lie limp
or bleed?

Succession

Genesis

As gilded leaves of history will tell
through memory dendritic in their veins
the height and heft of forest knew its form
before it first expressed itself to Stone,
and so when granite walls inquired of trees
of birth and death and interstitial space
the mighty forest boasted in reply,
'Not one day lived that did not feel my hand,
nor one night slept beneath another's leaves.'
And Stone paternal knew this much was true,
immutable in arboreal spans;
that molecules exist within themselves
but watersheds of eons, days and years
are strung with binding energy of grain
concentric rings, as year dissolves to year
as ripples from a stone tossed in the pond
preceded by as many as may come
from seed or just the someday of a seed
to patient fertile earth that takes and gives
the life, the veins of water through the rings
which all as one persist as Brother Time.

Old Growth

A patient grove, all amnesty for green
more verdant once than sprucewine it becomes
now darkened by its own authentic shade

that carefully selects which light may pass
by virtue of its dappling intellect
and its innate ability to see
the rounded stone from one that must abide
within the stream until its purest thoughts
are laminar, wood grain as it would flow
when its hydrology professes faith.
Each eon yields its captains and its saints
and modest stout omniciencies in groves
whose erudite rebuttal to the storm
can see the rain as next day's soft repast
and yield to reformation, unlike stone
as water in obeisance upward flows,
its Mecca the charisma of the trees.

Inheritance

How is it then that capillary curves
beneath the surface of the light may hide
the brush strokes of the artist, Brother Time
who scripts the laminar effusions which
cannot exist until in elegy?
When statuary then recumbent lies
and circular geometries are planed
to water shadows turning over stones
the grain, a perfect circle told in lines—
I ask suspended currents in the ice
whose composition is both form and dream
invisible, released when life agrees

at last to change of phase, its latent heat—
Is energy imparted or infused?
The answer may abide in tabletops
or fence posts which, in homage, know their past
contained within the prayerful shapes of fields.

Generations

A sapling, genome, life's encrypted veins
arising verdant fractals of the ones
who left their leaves but never take their leave,
instructions printed into every palm
that reaches from the soil that imparts
a tree in whole upon each trembling leaf,
the heirloom premonition of a form
in early hands unfolding just to glimpse
the stature of before and yet to be,
and quiet, in a womb beneath the bark
decisions of the hue and pulp and grain
are patiently already made as glyphs
to wait while aspirations turn to shade
within this fellowship of hands upturned
and outward stretched in bold arterial faith
that glade already turns again to grove,
the will and affirmation of the field's
conception of a rhythmic arbor rune—
though pine or birch may dream in maple red
of kingdoms from a seed in vapor's eye,
the stone in walls beneath communes with Time

and knows the ebb of vision in a space,
that while its lineage awaits, it must
its own invented shades imagine first.

Honor

Which bugle blast will call them to their ranks,
with all the weight and burthen of their day
upon their shoulders, cinched with hemp rope tight?
A generation's avant-garde unknown
unborn among the ranks of footmen proud
of every unity they may defend.
They march into their Gettysburg to stand,
if only to become a field themselves,
a sepulcher of lineage from sprig
to branch to limb to trunk and into roots,
the soldier falls as all who came before
enshrining them and those who yet may be
that fire, timber, warmth and strength be theirs,
a freedom that translates itself as smoke
from barrens scorched to homestead and to steam
as latent heat or dormant grain opine
that only in submission may be known
the dignity of woodland laid to rest.

Ascension

Descendants' skin is tempered by the fate
of absence and the strength that it conceals

as wan imagination's sawdust spire
will calcify toward an aspiration
rising ruddier and more sublime

with God-sent hubris and naivety
that renders history in pastel pale
and sculpts a temple seen but once a year
where prayers of intercession ring by ring
request of Time enough but which to rise
and lift the forbear spirit from its field
that fueled the factories and rails and hearth,
now watered yet again by falling leaves
ancestral but which breathe and pulse the same
as brethren, parent, patriarchal form
who rose a thousand years or maybe ten,
yet rose and rise with pulmonary lust.
They know the harbingers of time to fall
a purpose tempered by its c'est la vie
and certainty that its majestic form
is printed not on just its every leaf
but also in the prescience of its seed.

About the Author

Kirk Westphal's poetry reflects his life's work and his reverence for waters and the forests that protect them. He is an environmental consultant who advises government agencies around the world on water management, and who is also currently building a timber frame cabin on a remote trout stream in the hills of Western Massachusetts. He has won national awards for professional journal articles on water management and is working on another book on the restoration of a small patch of forest. He is a frequent contributor to *Dunes Review*, and his poems have also appeared in *The Road Not Taken* and *Albatross*. He was a winner of the Plein Air Poetry Contest sponsored by the Fruitlands Museum in Massachusetts in 2012 and has read a comic poem about his boyhood idols, the Chicago Cubs, on National Public Radio. His first book, **No Ordinary Game**, a celebration of great moments in sports that happen to everyday people, was published by Rowman and Littlefield in June of 2015. He lives between an orchard and a lake in Stow, Massachusetts.

Photo courtesy of Nancy Gould Photography

www.ingramcontent.com/pod-product-compliance
Lightning Source LLC
Chambersburg PA
CBHW071105090426
42737CB00013B/2484